Dark Matter

Also by Christopher Buckley

Blue Autumn (Copper Beech, 1990)
*Blossoms & Bones: On the Life and Work
    of Georgia O'Keefe* (Vanderbilt, 1988)
Dust Light, Leaves (Vanderbilt, 1986)
Other Lives (Ithaca House, 1985)
Last Rites (Ithaca House, 1980)

DARK MATTER

Poems by
Christopher Buckley

Christopher Buckley

For Peter —
with thanks &
admiration for
your fine work —
Chris

Copper Beech Press

ACKNOWLEDGMENTS

Black Warrior Review: "Days of Black and White"; *The Gettysburg Review:* "Speculation in Dark Air," "Beauty in the World"; *The Hudson Review:* "After Another War"; *The Iowa Review:* "Dark Matter," "Serenade in Blue," "Sun Spots"; *The Kenyon Review:* "After a Theme by Vallejo, After a Theme by Justice"; *The Missouri Review:* "Tabula Rasa"; *New England Review:* "Seasonal"; *Passages North:* "Star Journal"; *Poet Lore:* "Prima Facie"; *Poetry:* "Dark Time," "Midlife," "Apologues of Winter Light," "Perseid Meteor Shower," "Isotropic," "Reincarnation"; *Poetry Miscellany:* "Death's White Spaces"; *Seneca Review:* "Pange Lingua"; *The Sewanee Review:* "Leaving the West Coast," "Day After Christmas."

Grateful acknowledgment is made also to the Poetry Society of America for the Gertrude B. Claytor Memorial Award for "Sun Spots" and to Pushcart Press for including "Apologues of Winter Light" and "Sun Spots" in *The Pushcart Prize: Best of the Small Presses, XV* and *XVI.*

Special thanks to Gary Young, Nadya Brown, Jon Veinberg, and Gary Soto for their support and help with these poems; to the Fulbright Committee, the Ucross Foundation, and the State System of Higher Education of the Commonwealth of Pennsylvania for the time and opportunity to write some of these poems; and to the Deans of Arts & Sciences of West Chester University for a grant that helped make this book possible.

Cover: "Spirals," © 1992 by Geanna Merola. Photograph by Erik Landsberg.

For information, address the publisher:
      Copper Beech Press
      English Department
      Box 1852
      Brown University
      Providence, Rhode Island 02912

Library of Congress Cataloging-in-Publication Data
Buckley, Christopher, 1948-
    Dark matter : poems / by Christopher Buckley. — 1st ed.
      p. cm.
    ISBN 0-914278-62-2 (pbk. : alk. paper) : $9.95
    I. Title.
PS3552.U339D37   1993
811'.54—dc20

93-4138
CIP

Set in Bembo by Louis Giardini
Printed and bound by McNaughton & Gunn
First Edition
Manufactured in the United States of America

In memory of William H. Buckley (1920-1991)

CONTENTS

I

II

I

SERENADE IN BLUE

> *Where is the sea, that once solved the whole loneliness*
> *Of the Midwest?*
>
> James Wright

Because my father knew that loneliness, that tedium in a breeze
slip-streaming behind his Oldsmobile and bending back sleepy heads
of blackeyed susans along the interstate as he moved around
all those years — station to radio station, remote broadcast to broadcast —
he brought me to the Pacific where the sea's blue notes scaled the cliffs
and salt air, where the white gulls lolled day-long on the sprindrift light
as wind pulled apart the surf and offered it up — foam-flowers and song
as signs of grace, as means and end — into my arms . . .
                                                    But I should begin
with silence and 1942, the sky over the Atlantic at dusk, two swaths
of blue-deep water and dimming air banded like an Ohio Blue Tip match,
one that he keeps in his shirt pocket and flicks to light his Lucky Strikes,
which is appropriate, for he is from Ohio, steaming east at four knots tops
on the *John C. Calhoun,* a "Liberty Ship," meaning some sorry freighter
overloaded with men and supplies. He knows they're virtual sitting ducks
for U-boats, though they zigzag forty-eight days to Takerati and the Gold
Coast of Africa, but feels almost fortunate, knowing they carry lumber below and
above deck, figuring they might float if hit. Sitting out on deck as night
comes down, lights out, no smoking allowed, he sees clear to the curved
horizon where ships are going up like the flare of matches struck against
the dark.
        He's not thinking of the life behind, of his father wearing down
in a shoe factory in Washington Court House or those boys gone off
to college and football in Columbus, gone to Pensacola for Air Cadets,
he doesn't even give a thought to that neighbor girl with a solid backhand
and her own tennis court, the balmy aroma of grass splashed and hover-
ing on the air as his first serve *thwacks* in . . . He's not even envisioning
wings — the wings on the Sphinx because they are headed for Cairo, wings
on human-headed bulls at the Assyrian gate because the beard he will grow
in the desert will have him looking like an Assyrian, and because the bulls
are said to bring good luck;
                            no, he's humming one of Glenn Miller's sweetest
orchestrations, remembering where the vocalist comes in, thinking of bands
he sang with in Miami and Chillicothe. For the whole war, he's got it
in his head, even while he and Howard, his one home-town friend, swim
untouched amid schools of barracuda in Takerati Bay, bounce their DC-3,
landing *with* the wind, or navigate to Ascension Island so they can refuel

on the round trip to South America — a rock in the South Atlantic others knew they'd missed when that big bass beat in their engines died and they headed for the soundless center of the sea.

He'd never heard of Clarinda, Iowa, before Miller's plane sank into the blue between London and Paris. He was stateside in time for Christmas, calling home with a telegram that said Howard was killed on a last instruction flight, a day before discharge; and his mother, who had never heard of such things, had gone to answer the doorbell, and there was Howard in his astral body, floating in an azure light, and so she said she knew.

He began then to think about the future, a family, decided to study radio and give up singing. Yet I see him, the way I think he will always see himself, after that last time he sang with a band — stepping up to the standing microphone, his right hand cupped over his ear as he picked up the trombone's fading cue to croon, *When I hear that "Serenade in Blue," I'm somewhere in another world, alone, with you . . .*

BEAUTY IN THE WORLD

(Washington Court House, 1954)

Outside, the occasional Studebaker gleamed
down the wide and endless streets, through
a half-light and humidity that was all of Ohio —
residential elms in their unwavering torpor,
the shade flush and indistinguishable from
the cement porch where there was nothing
much for me to do visiting my Aunt Valeska . . .

Most of the day she disappeared to the basement
where she had a beauty parlor word of mouth,
where her regulars drifted in day long through
an unmarked door at the bottom of the drive.
First time I ventured down there, my eyes teared
from a cloud of ammonia flooding upstairs
as permanent wave solutions were applied.

Five or six, I didn't know what to think
of that or the glossy cream-and-chocolate walls,
the phosphorescent lights that blinked and hummed,
squads of spring-like, wire rollers in formation
on ascending trays, the galvanized finger-length
clips that twittered and pincurled the women's hair.

Nor were things any clearer when Mother's auburn
pony tail turned brassy red, or when I saw a woman,
wrapped to the chin with towels and a plastic bib,
let her head fall back into my aunt's hands and dis-
appear through a wide V in the sink.
                                  So I'd stack
boxes of her Roux Dye into towers, and stare up
at women with nets hugging a galaxy of curlers
and clips to their heads as they took up stations
under the row of dryers, which looked, to my mind,
like monstrous behives — tan or pink, they were
attached to matching plastic chairs with chrome
tubes, and locked down into place leaving only
the eyes visible as a thick electric buzz built up.
For over an hour they sat there lost in LIFE or
PHOTOPLAY, some flicking Old Golds or L&Ms

into standing ashtrays, unable to hear me pester
about where they lived, their children my age,
what exactly it was that was going on in there?

A concrete floor was painted iron-red all the way
to the dark storage cupboard in the back, but I was
to stay on the rubber mats, near where my aunt
clipped and curled, near the swivel chair and sink
where she worked a black hose and her fingers in,
chatted with women barely visible beneath it all,
and kept one eye out for me. I counted clouds
and shoes shuffling past the transom windows
where the square sky was nothing new, waved
goodbye to ladies who were pleasant despite
all they had been put through.
                                              That was the early
50's, 3rd Street in a town smaller than Chillicothe.
Those were the standing years exacting a price
from my aunt's legs, the rinses and the tints burning
her hands until she wore her felt driving gloves
every time she went out, and the Rhinegold beers
at night with her one friend, Bernie, who under-
wrote insurance, washed nothing away but the last
days of the home beauty parlor trade.
                                              Now there was TV,
Toni Home Perms with those pink, spongy curlers,
now women would drive downtown to places with neon
signs and checked linoleum tiles, places where
the new bouffants and pageboys were displayed
in window fronts, and where no kid bounced curlers
down the basement stairs or sat late afternoons
beneath one of those ominous helmets looking out
to paint-blistered walls, clicking a dead switch
in the dark, alone for a little while longer
with the lost mysteries of beauty in the world.

DAYS OF BLACK AND WHITE

Still, they come back clearly,
unfocused and myopic as they were —
the cold eye of the CBS insignia zooming
out of the dark as we opened
the Sylvania's console doors,
or each Monday, the catechism responses
like dark brick layered down the page —
all the arbitrary and two-dimensional vision
of those days . . .
            The rush of it all
was thick and impossible to penetrate
as that marine layer of fog we wandered
our way through to class each day,
our checkered uniform shirts blue-grey
as the chafed, wind-dull winter sea
where the rote and repetition of the hours
were out-shouted by the waves.
                One day
the nun marched a bunch of boys
from the blacktop and tether ball,
the skull and crossbones of her habit
waving over a sun-slick field where we were
to trace out a diamond and wear away the weeds —
this portion of the world, we were told, was ours
and no one else could interfere. So we felt
no sea change churning then beneath the oblique
surface of the times, or especially in our sleep-
walking blood . . .
         The parents like Ike,
the House Un-American Activities Committee
had made movies safe, and the Church flaunted
its Index of forbidden books. Our lives
came under the tutelage of nuns whose grasp
of the world was manifest in the thunderbolt
spearing St. Theresa's ecstatic heart,
in the sanctuary defiler struck down and burning
on the spot, or in the boy who, smuggling
a communion wafer home and floating it
on water, poked it with a fork to find blood . . .
These were the true uses of the mind

and so far as we knew formed the shining
perspective of the soul against darkness
in this life.
                    And though we suspected
most of what we'd heard was far from fact,
we understood it when the black-and-white photo
of the Crab Nebula in our eighth grade text
was described as a cloud of light the color
of rose petals appearing in the peasant's serape
as he stood beneath the Virgin of Guadalupe —
that scene on the dry cleaning calendar
with its gold and starry border tacked
to the coatroom in back of class.
                              We had no idea
this would be the end of things as we knew
or would ever know them. That spring,
we were squared off final period across
the linoleum tiles, forced to count out
fox trot and waltz. We wore clip-on ties
and the poplin suits our mothers bought
almost proudly at J.C. Penney's; girls balanced
in heels and dresses of unnatural gold
or minty green, dresses so stiff with starch
and petticoats they rustled like newspapers
with the least spin or twirl.
                          We'd been aching
to get at them all year, but now at arm's length
and half the time in gloves — and even when we were
allowed some rock and roll to head off a shuffled anarchy
or stomped rebellion — we were joyless, awkward
in our scuffed and embarrassed shoes . . .
                                        True,
Alan Shepard had been hurled headlong
into space, but Sputnik was now years old —
fewer mysteries were explained by a saint's
sudden levitation above the assembled masses in Peru.
Now we had Kennedy and were going for the moon;
the world was shrinking into its last three-quarters-size prints
taken with our Kodak Star Mites the night of graduation:
girls in their armored dresses, boys in business suits

with the pervasive evidence of safety razors —
constellations of small red stars on cheek and chin —
photos snapped walking out of the auditorium,
eyes wide a last time — into the flash — aspiring
to what we knew would be the future where our hair
could be slicked back with Brylcreem or held aloft
by laquered waves of spray.
                              I remember
staying up that night, the test pattern's wheel
and one note, and how, as it was turned off,
the picture shrank to a dot of light tunneling
into the tube. The last image that came
to mind as I drifted off on the davenport
was of Parents' Night during my first year
in the school where I'd just spent most of my life . . .
The old school house stood next to the new
stucco rooms, and it was used as theater and stage;
the nuns had organized a Minstrel Show.
Looking out the windows into that spring sky,
stars stood out like little pats of butter
on the deep and comfortable blue, and because
this was the 50's and no one was thinking
of anyone but themselves, and because we were
brought up to do precisely as we were told,
the older boys delivered jokes out front
while, with the whole of the second grade,
I waited in the back in overalls and kerchief,
in black-face with white gardening gloves
on my hands, to be called out
dancing and smiling for the final number.

PANGE LINGUA

Pange Lingua gloriosi
corporis mysterium
Sanguinisque pretiosi
Quem in mundi pretium

I remember the lost angels
and the cosmologies of that war in clouds,
the black flags of their wings aflame
ten feet above our astonished heads,
how archangels gained footholds on the air
as swords shimmered with the terrible
light of their steel-blue eyes, and how,
as slides changed on the suspended screen,
the very edge of heaven caught fire
with the projector's glow — and the fall
from grace was swift and sure, silent,
and far below anywhere
we would ever see on earth.
       Then the nun
in her death-black habit covered the lens
with her left hand and held forth at length
on our iniquity, our concupiscent hearts
and their weakness for the dark abyss floating
just barely beneath our feet.
        She railed on
about the flesh, the danger in those temporal
and intemperate rags, the vestments of desire
that would be left to the purifying coals
before we could ascend the light's long stem
and be allowed to wear that starry crown.

And this was everlasting, running on despite
the ringing of a bell that should have freed us
to lunch tables and the fields. And it persisted
year to year as we marched the sandstone steps
to church and were reminded with a cross of ash
on our foreheads, or bone-white candles crossed
before our throats; and always one or two in front
looked momentarily like tiny saints in trance
before fainting dead away from incense,
a low cloud of it curling from the altar
like a plague in that film by Cecil B. DeMille.

We were forbidden to look out the windows
at jacarandas eloquent with wind, at the starless
limits of our weedy thoughts, at the oxalis
and loquat blooms resplendent with sun,
for even the clouds slid dutifully into place
above the hills like all of us in uniform shirts
filing grade by grade into pews each month
to make the Nine First Fridays and so guarantee
a last-ditch chance to recant our sins and slip in
under heaven's gate. We processed, flower girls
and all, singing the *Pange Lingua* — Aquinas's hymn
to the Blessed Sacrament — a redundant lilt of Latin
learned an unconscious morpheme at a time
until it so soaked our minds we could recite it
in our sleep.
    Thus we were to forego the present
mystery in our lives, the shot wings of light
spinning in our bodies and our blood when,
in the purple evening after mass, we were left
to ourselves while parents and priests took coffee;
we ran in the three-quarter's dark over the black-
topped yard, tagging those in white most easily
or hiding against the hedge's dark green flames,
the blood hot in our cheeks — or one last May,
behind the classroom walls, a first time burning
in someone else's arms, and that cobalt sky
spewing stars like petals thrown along the aisles,
like a thousand hosts we were never to touch.

     *   *

And so it was with angels and our chorusing
to whatever ever-after, until almost all the trees
vanished from that yard, the tables and fields
turned small, transpired into another life.
And the whole earth smaller in its turn,
and the wars coming down out of the clouds
to our living rooms with a vision of how the world
might end — the salvage of all our days amounting
to little more than leaves or long grasses in the half-
life and steady attrition of a breeze.

                                    And when
it comes to stars will we still be singing,
and what song might be ours when the lungs
have taken on that sea-colored dust that coats
the olive boughs, or the heart that darkness
inside the olive's skin? On that day I pray
I'm being driven down East Valley Road where
I am once more pointing out the Spanish palms,
sun-laced pimientos, and pepper-scented pines —
where in June beneath a bronzed shag of eucalyptus
I'll find the blazing trumpet vines, and slowing
by the school yard wall, I'll breathe the free
verses of that air and still believe the mockingbird
offers up the bright body of his song for me.

STAR JOURNAL

Astronomy is for the soul —
                    the truth about what
                              and who we are
                                        and will be.
The universe grinding blithely away
                              and we, reflective grist, stellar pollen
cooling down enough to somewhere
                    finally shine —
                              a caucus of dust and acids blown
over the warped table of space,
                    arriving on the shirttails of comets to lap down
on tundra, settle on
          palmetto leaves, blinking above an isthmus white with sand. . .
                              *

And so unconsciously we take our breaths
                              into orbit about the solar apparatus
of the heart —
                    star with its own fusion and collapse — each measure and molecule
voluble but
                    unaccountable in a code
                              comprising even the weightless freight
of thought
                    as we stand out each night exhaling
                              dim clouds from the ghosted
wing-span of our lungs . . .
                              *

We have built machines
                    that can see light burning
                              from the lost beginning —
faint quasars, a print-out just coming
                              through the hazed background buzz
after fifteen billion years.
                              *

From our vantage point in the outer precincts,
                              we tune in radio from the first
broadcast, big downbeat still on every network
                              and starry frequency

as we go for a spin through the galactic plasma,
                                        a kind of Dyna-Flow along
the boulevards,
                    oxbows and sluice gates of time . . .

                                *

Telescopes *are* time machines —
                        lanes for recovered light
                                            bringing the past
up to speed,
                pulling down the crystal spheres
                                        and broken symmetries,
                                                        exposing
our surroundings, our irrepressible, elemental histories
                                            with which we continue
to negotiate
                as if the wheel were firmly in our hands . . .

                                *

Space itself is slipping away,
                        expanding,
                                    but into what?
                                        Aristarchus of Samos, against
Ptolemy and the popular astrophysics, deduced
                        that earth was a planet, that stars were very far
away indeed!
                A little over 2,000 years
                                    and this information was confirmed.
                                        Still, there is the black
frame of space,
                stars untrue in our parallax view — their bent scintillations
                                                    so many curve balls
breaking at the last instant over the outside corner
                                        of the plate —
                                and so our doubt about everything
published above us in the dark —
                            and then the blank and sweeping margins of the east
each dawn
                after we've again tried to decipher the shorthand in the night.

                                *

Sitting up at dawn, starlings appear
                              across the lawn like black holes in the mist-
bright sheen.
              Birds congregate, begin a cappella — cavatinas and recitatives —
without the least
                  introspection, time-management or stress,
                                              neither do they sew . . .
A steady disregard of the attrition in the air,
                              the ambiguous blue going of the world —
something like a rose-colored nebula
                          boiling in their breasts, moving them
to praise no matter the implications,
                      the copyright of the cold.

                              *

The lawn sprinklers whirl out their silver
                              and unerring loops . . .
                                                  Gravity
keeps us here,
              the weak force and the strong force,
                                        the invisible and
the dissembled something in the unified field —
                              even as light is fused
and driven through charged tines of air,
                          torching the tree, black *Y* against
the mustard sky, wringing out the horizon,
                          ash of its arms extended — funnel cloud
taking farm house and Ford Galaxy sedan
                          up the violet ascension of the sky
against that gravity and half the Midwest
                      on the TV A.M. news, particles accelerated,
snowy dots of channels flipped through.
                              Out the window, the glitter in the night
river washed away, discord of black
                      sand rolling over some last bright bones —
wing bones, let's say,
                  holding it all up
                              about us as we reel outward,
                                              carrying

our blue and parochial atmosphere with us,

                                    our little argument advanced

against all the blind stuff of space,

                        the dark matter now ninety per cent of everything,

denser than anthracite with time,

                            dead energy so massed it will never shine,

nor harbor one mote of mica,

                    one iced diamond-fleck

                              not inked and unknowable.

Only its gravitational arcs, its fingerprints hold

                        the pearl-like and whirling

Milky Way in thrall, keep the arms swirled

                        brilliantly together, rotating in sync

with the yolky center, edges bright

                    with the hum and singing of atoms swimming

outward, burning away

              somewhere nothing ends.

ISOTROPIC

after the launching of the Hubble Space Telescope, April 25, 1990

Looked at in different directions,
the universe shows no significant
difference in its general appearance —
no blue shifts, nothing coming our way,
no change imminent; everything's red-shifted
and rotating outward, bright arm over arm
in the same expanding sea . . .

It's as if we've been standing
at the bottom of a pool, looking up
at the rippling colors and flights of birds,
the way we've had to chart and ponder
heavenly bodies beaming down to us
through stardust and patinas of our air.

Now a new observatory runs laps beyond
our atmosphere, copestone on that breathless ledge
of black — its floating beryllium eye
fixed on the unedited ticker-tape of light,
those naked lines exponentially deconstructing
in their own non stop play back of the past,
their medium the only message
about a point in time beyond any point
in time and that undoing that set things
spinning on the logarithm of the dark.

And though the new thinking sees it all
without the chaotic and misleading sprawl
of motes that's underwritten our reasoning
for so long and saved us from considering
a serious connnection to design, some cataract
across the lens, it appears, will keep
this finally from us for yet a little while.

But even when the unfiltered news comes through,
is it likely we'll undergo a sea change,
so to speak, and find a bright new continent
at the heart of it instead of the one
we've been sailing for all along?

When I look up to the plaster and ceiling beams,
water-damaged from another season's rains,
I see amber ellipses and tea-colored swirls,
which, drifting toward the window and the wall,
look like dried roses or, equally, like nebulae
with their dense palm-print and smudge of suns.

Yet birds still slipstream on their magnetic,
star-gazed routes, and still the prevailing winds
pause a little and allow that cider scent of autumn
to loiter on the afternoon — the high western sky
reading left to right as always, and the blue
tree dahlias corresponding —
                                        then the horizon
spills out like a glass of light and dust, the violet
overtones finely invisible as our breath
as we sit smiling among the fallen leaves,

collars turned up around our necks as we stare
inefficiently toward our old constabulary of stars,
that same light we've seen all along,
light which will one day rise
through our shoulder blades and arms
and set us blindly off, more white and weightless
than the air we leave behind.

DEATH'S WHITE SPACES

for Rick and Jane

The only thing you remember is your life.
Neruda

We detour off the road to Bled
and stop beneath a canopy
of trees, two tall rows of chestnuts
little more than a man's length apart
and all ivory with blooms in May.
A gravel path leads through them
up a hill, and a fine grey dust,
like someone's lost thought,
lifts and floats back behind
some nurses and those walking
on their arms for nothing
more than the steady exhalation
of plants and light . . .

The clinic here adjoins
a small museum, a white-
washed row of cells that seem,
at first, as harmless
as the terrycloth robes inmates wear
as they wander about the grounds.
But each cubicle is preserved
with photographs, with artifacts
of iron and the tortured
paragraphs that spare you nothing
recounting Nazi methods and effects.

Plexiglass protects the walls
where someone carved a candle
inside a heart, some little light
left to burn through that dark;
and one etched "Rada" — love's name
or the love of defiance in the face
of such death — using God-knows-what
for fingernails, given the starvation
which somehow did not dull
their anger or their will.

Patients saunter down the corridor
in slippers, in their cloud-soft robes,
in and out of that last room,
the one with the three great stakes
used to string partisans up
for days in the yard; they stroll
outside, unconsciously across
the unmowed field where they pick
the weeds for anything they're worth
beneath the blooming sun.

I follow them into the raw light
of noon, unable now to close my eyes
to a dream recurring all my early life . . .

> *In a country dark with conifers,*
> *I'm in another body*
> *I always recognize as mine —*
> *in regular fatigues two friends and I*
> *belly-crawl down toward the river,*
> *thinking we can slip away by night*
> *despite barbed wire and the manic dogs.*
> *Then the search lamps, automatic fire*
> *and tracers open up, and I black out*
> *with the stars dissolving on the water . . .*

Near the parking lot, my friend
points out a pillbox almost hidden
among purple irises — he tells me
the Germans let prisoners think
escape was possible, routinely
left a door open so they'd break
across the night-blue fields
with the white tatter of their shirts
making them look like moths
scattered from a lawn. They'd struggle
up the slope where it always seemed
untroubled and green, where birds
were always going over the sleeping
branches of the trees; but before

the woods were ever reached,
the machine gun cut them
in half like flowers — ten partisans
for every German taken in the town —
just as they saw the first white
limits of sky lift above the high
and distant arms of pines . . .

    Slovenia

AFTER ANOTHER WAR

In the museum now
they've finally got the heads
on straight.
        A few years back
in Wyoming, when drought
exposed a cave bottom
submerged beyond all memory,
complete and intact frames
were pulled to light
from the deep and oil-dark mud —
they realized then
that even for dinosaurs
they'd had the wrong,
too-large skulls
all this time
on the great assemblages
and city block of bones . . .

And today, as pine martins
and house finches peck in order
on the back porch for seeds,
I'm reminded of the PBS show
pointing out their fierce pre-
possessing legs and beaks,
the scaled-down millennia
and slow, reconstituted architecture
of wings that brought us
to the fact that birds are about all
that remain . . .
        And recently
in Tuscany, in the red limestone
in back of Gubbio, two scientists,
father and son, tracked down
a layer of sedimentary carbon
so impacted with stardust
for the feather-thinness
of the band, that it attested to
a conflagration two million years ago:
a bright and terrible falling
from the sky that so shagged

the air with dust and cut off
light, it coldly choked
the great beasts out.
                    Only these
sized-down models survived,
who, once the smoke had cleared,
took to the air and trees in fear
of us and our big emerging brains,
and who, for no good reason
it seems, still sing to us
as life is taken steadily
down another notch.

PERSEID METEOR SHOWER

Out late in the wide dark field,
                          looking into the domed wide dark,
a moonless sky clearer even than
                          the planetarium from our air-
brushed and illuminated youth,
                          we spotted Cassiopeia, its <u>W</u> pointing
like lamp posts to Perseus
                          and there that black window
through which meteors
                          would rain down. For a minute, only
blank incessant space
            fell through,
                          then faintly we could see
the misty band of the Milky Way
                          turning with us
                                      as our fingers
on the air traced the Northern Cross,
                          the Big Dipper's steely pan
before the jazzy, unsynched bursts
                          and strings of flame cross-hatched
the circuit board of stars.
                The thickest yellow streaks and burns
were like wooden safety matches
                          pulled parallel over the horizon
and hill's slow length —
                then a few high darts like sparks popping off
welding with acetylene.
                In two hours, the sky ignited with something
like thirty shooting stars,
                and my Dutch friend recalled that in Amsterdam
last year
            a meteorite the size of a briquet broke through a family's roof
and cooled in a bowl of soup —
                          other pieces, they figured, pockmarked
the Siberian snow.
                Between flashes, we guessed at their blazing cause,
then moved on to
                Einstein's matter and traveling light — and there,
invisible
            in that dark space, it was almost as if we weren't

                                        made up of both
or diminished by the distance of the stars. We only knew
                                        that we were moving
outward, away from each other,
                        toward no place we could name, with the
                        view
to our galaxy's jeweled heart
                        kept from us, dimmed by a starry dust cloud
dense in Sagittarius.
                        But, while things seemed set
                                above us, it was magnificent
to find a place in this cold and abstract whirl
                                and take what fire we were given.

                                        Ucross, Wyoming

SUN SPOTS

Every eleven years they appear
like dark pores beneath the floating
photosphere, the atomic skin that makes
up the surface. The *auroras* erupt then, too,
the irrepressible fiery hair of the sun torn loose and
thrown into space at us, a welter of flaming astral birds
lifting off the *limb*, that visible edge and hard limit of the star.
The magnetic whorls, paired anywhere from two to fifty, are then
several times larger than earth, and strain and pull at fission's invisible frame,
setting out against the rotation of burning equatorial seas, hovering above the blue-
hot center like a sickness in gravity. Yet, when the ocellated torrents and latitudinal drifts
are graphed, the *penumbras* echo the winged patterns of butterflies rather than some matrix of sinking
anti-matter. And after all our spinning about this source, this seething theme and variation, we have nothing new
to say about the spots outside of the old tales that still flare up and forebode havoc in the distant atmosphere of our lives.
So last winter when auroras blazed and the black fields swelled, it was no wonder that broadcasts were interrupted
with blank bursts. "Live from the Met," waffled out and in with a certain nothing on the air —
a soundless hiss and drop-out from the skies. And just weeks before, the opera at the Met
went, a first time ever, unfinished — and the stage turned dark after one un-
balanced soul threw himself mid-aria from a balcony to a break-
neck death. And so, the dread forecasts must have held
sway over at least one man as his will sparked
out and reason fumed in on itself.

It was reported he'd recently
been observed storming around
the mezzanine, stalking some absent
space — and with the house lights down he slipped
into the empty box and pitched himself head-long over
into the dark. He did not stand out in tuxedo and black tie,
they said — there was no sound, no note. Only the lovely and loveless
Turandot, waiting high and star-white on the stage, with her riddle for the hero
who was confident as any tenor despite the heads of other suitors who'd been unable to answer
staggered about her on poles like disjunct planets, like moons bruised beyond all aspects of the light . . .
Is it coincidence then that this year they've discovered the hole in our ozone to be much larger than first supposed,
that melanoma is on the rise, that the clear-cut Amazon is leaving us with thin air, a simmering rain?
Where finally on the scale are we — galactic to sub-atomic? Our cells cluster and spiral
like galaxies, to or from what effect? Yet we're most open to what lies beyond us —
astronomers have now abandoned our own solar system in favor of great radio
telescopes fixed on the obfuscated heart of space — steely petals of the dishes
unfolding, like camera lenses, like slow and awkward flowers
craning toward sound instead of light. And anchored
firmly in those white sands and eroding shoals
of time, they focus toward some innuendo
sung down in dim, binomial bleeps —
too far away ever to be of use
to the future hanging fire.

PRIMA FACIE

I've always liked the old story of Bertrand Russell
giving a public lecture on astronomy, and a woman
standing up afterwards to say it was all rubbish,
that the earth was really flat and supported
on the back of a giant tortoise! And when Russell
asked just what the turtle was standing on,
the woman was ready and replied, "Why, it's turtles
all the way down."
                    Doesn't it add up this flawlessly
while we take our short swim off these rocks —
stunned in the immediate and febrile good will
of the light as it replays every summer
traveling home from the shore, green sea
still sparkling in our veins, horizon's blue frame
holding, crepuscular, one star only burning
there and inside of us in continuous disputation
of the dark . . .
                    And again this evening I'm watching
a feckless delegation of clouds depart for home
or perhaps the rain-emptied coast of Dieppe, I'm brooding
on immortality where white sandwich wrappers
lifted above those chalk-dull cliffs and seagulls argued
low along a flinty sea blown back along the quai
as if there were another element to the light that we,
stalled there and as simple as those wind-thinned trees,
were letting slip away . . .
                    A circus had cleared off
overnight, and papers scuttled on the long green field,
a red-and-yellow poster waving from a bench, were little
to say time and space had been put to use there and then,
and in that way — unremarkable now and shuffling off
with the salt shifting of the air.
                    A wafer of sun
cut across the clouds' grey scroll, the black edges
of night bleeding in until bright specks floated up
on the blank plate of space with all our unsupported
paradigms for science and for art — the dark ocean
spattered with refracted light like the grainy surface
of the soul — both perhaps expanding, still being etched
with the lost music of the spheres — while we were only
at sea again in our hearts, pointing out first-hand the old
shapes and overlappings, the sure and selfsame stars.

II

LEAVING THE WEST COAST

(after Cavafy)

When suddenly you wake to shouts and music
rising from the street — someone's convertible
top down, quad stereo up all the way —
it is too late to mourn for plans gone
wrong, the life that is abandoning you.
Just as there are always the unaccountable
clouds, dull silverware of the moon, shunting
over the hills, so too there is something
tuneless in sun-burned eucalyptus leaves,
in stars salted obliquely over the sea.
For now, looking out to stars, it takes little
to say they've failed you, to fault your luck
turned black — or there, in that one thick
cluster to the north, to point out the dogs
of academe, the bright tossing of the bones.

And in the drive, a rented truck gleams
like the promise of riches in the east —
two more hours and you cross the desert
by night as if carrying something stolen,
as if the gods ever slept. Isn't it useless
to plead before the moon, to wish things
otherwise? Instead, as one who has seen
this coming all along, nod with emotion
to the dry rose canes and amaryllis,
to every illusion likewise laid bare.

Take your courage out on the balcony while
the star jasmine still breathes for you
into this dream-deep sky. But above all,
don't fool yourself, don't say it was a dream —
not the Spanish villas and red tile roofs,
not the violet air of jacarandas above the streets,
nor lemon blossoms riding a salt breeze
like some lost afternoon of love.
                                   It was good
to have been given such a city, this city
you're losing now, for truly you were not
deceived unless you let yourself believe

that bromide about the inheritance of the meek.
You made a living. You were worthy
of sun-stropped days, the azurite bay
calm with the slowed motion of sailing boats
as you drank white wine on Wednesdays
from the deck of the restaurant — palm fronds
going blue, the street lamps pearl-like
in a string beyond the breakwater and the pier.

Look out now on the extravagant procession
of the night — a two-toned '59 Bel Air idling
at the light, at the wheel someone you once knew —
say goodbye as his tail lights dissolve into the dark.
Goodbye as well to streets full of European cars
the colors of money or champagne, to red and white
umbrellas, the Mexican beach cafes — goodbye
even to the generally drunken noise downstairs —
the young waiters, the speculators in land, none
of whom will remember a thing, come morning.

Santa Barbara, 1987

SEASONAL

for Ernesto Trejo

Sun has polished the last
green from camphor leaves
and in these flagging afternoons
they give off a flat, white sheen for blocks.
Over the San Joaquin, a dust is rising
to follow the evening home . . .

And what will it mean if tonight,
above the failed September gardens,
stars fall over the starry suburbs where
once things looked fixed above us,
where our occupation seemed to be
pointing to the outlines of angels or of beasts
and, over wine, guessing out the long-term
business of the light, speaking fearlessly
of Time and Space in the detached
abstractions of scholars or saints,
speculating as if we, simply in the good will
and brilliance of our blood,
were going to outlast the sky?

We began with the immutable
backdrop of the west behind us, blue
eucalyptus climbing from the river
to that air, a cider-light filling in
the space between ash and pepper trees —
a few cumulus like ellipses at the horizon's end . . .

Now, as easily as bright wind or water
it's all escaped the purest gestures
of our arms — what wouldn't we give
to stand again in that common light of day?

Autumn's moving in with a scrum
of low clouds the color of old snow,
the color of the gauze around this life,
with whatever it is the past has
in its bowl after all its begging.
I only know it takes me

by the back of the neck,
and when it picks up enough
to bend the yellowed grass
and thick dry heads of clover back,
I stop short and wonder if it's you
I sometimes hear as I make my weak sense
of things — but honestly, my friend,
I wonder even more if it's my own name
now, there on the wind's rough lips.

TABULA RASA

And endless once again it will begin:
life that doesn't see, speak, or think . . .
Nazim Hikmet

If anything, it's only the wind
now that picks up our prayers
and carries them off to the sea
where it's usually March and hopes
float bluely across the surface
thorny with whitecaps there . . .

Then, we would practice for May
Procession, and so often as we
marched up the lightless center
of the church, our small hearts
spun purely as the invisible
rose petals flower-girls were
scattering along the sandstone aisle,
purely as the sun washing through
our arms from the one window
white with daylight all that way
up the air. And for this we were excused
from class, from fractions, long division
and the mental roadwork
of diagraming the compound-
complex sentence.
                        Still these nights,
the random punctuation of stars
keeps me from seeing exactly
how, with the fragments given us,
we can, with any certainty,
trace out the lines, the blue-
prints that reveal God's agreement
in it all. At best, far against the black,
there is some chalk dust of nebulae
a smeared hand print of light . . .

And though we now know better
than the old bearskins and bones,
the fact is that the universe, lock,
stock and expanding barrel, is red-

shifted and moving away from us,
from the fireball that sent every
primordial thing scuffling for its place
in the blank backwash of space.

Yet each time wild flowers appear
for which I have no names and
swallows weave about like algorithms
substantiating the structure of the skies,
I accept the old metaphors for life
like there's no tommorrow. Nonetheless,
there's all this dead air, untuned
radio on the frequency of the dark,
between us and our nearest neighbor
shining high in the tips of eucalyptus.
And beyond, the bright bent center
of the wheel, the anonymous read-out
that permits stars to become
the paradigms of our desire.

                    *

These days, I just look forward
to sitting back and breathing
among wild mustard weed and radish
bloom until I'm calm and reflective
as a cloud . . . and I remember then
sixth grade and Miss Vasquez,
the sky above La Paz in our geography book,
what it would be like . . . nothing
more than a chimney's ladder
of smoke anchoring that washed-out
blue, that clean slate waiting there;
the clouds, those old iconoclasts of sorrow,
sliding this way and that,
apparently above it all.
                              But then
that first-cut fragrance of grass
takes me to the foothills east of town,
where I'm kneeling on the blacktop
for the Angelus ringing from
Our Lady of Mt. Carmel,
for the seconds it takes to recite

the formula for all we believe.
I'm driving for a hoop as soon
as I've raced through lunch;
and not long after, cruising
in a Chevy Biscayne, putting a blue moon
and constellations to the test,
desperate for any physical
evidence of love among the wild
mint leaves and manic clips of time.

And now, at the end of autumn,
late in the afternoon, burning
that intensely on any account
almost makes sense as the days
draw short and the roses dry
to the color of old light, or skin —
and the wind that freshened
in the last sprays of leaves
seems to stream more forcefully
through the trees, through the channels
in the mind, scattering the silt there
with the grey and infinitesimal float
of stellar dust.
                        And evidently
the universe *was* once rolled
into a ball — quasars imploding,
a trillion stars boxed into one star's size.
Now nothing's more abstract or absent
with itself than these black
and starless holes where everything
might one day be thrown back
into the past. Now we know
that even when galaxies collide, suns
and planets escape as gas and galactic plasma
compress and collapse into a cloud
that can't be seen — we only blindly read it
there, pinpoint some faithless spot
where light's sucked over and erased,
much the way the voice is lost
as someone plummets down a waterfall,
though he's shouting into the white
and roaring air for everything he's worth.

DAY AFTER CHRISTMAS

for Francis Orsua

The wreath of della robbia breaks up
in wind, the peach tree is reduced to twig —
a last persimmon hangs like a bruised sun.
Last night, a friend and I put down a fifth
in shots with cash he'd saved to buy a tree;
we had agreed a tree would only die,
and pushing forty, sailed our own blue seas.
This morning air attacks my bloodshot eyes
as I watch Vandenberg fire missiles sky-
ward down the Pacific range — their trails fanned
out, lucent and veined as the wings of flies.
And shrill as cloistered nuns, mockingbirds chant
wry *Te Deum*'s above the frost-burnt yard —
everything comes exposed without regard.

REINCARNATION

There must be something.
James Wright

Outside our small sphere of influence, the orchestrations
of the universe are floating timelessly away — and inside,
a steady drift of particles is dusting down as if everything,
once shaken up, tumbles back inside this glassy globe
of space, rises and falls, snows around us forever, for as
long as we picture ourselves in this white and azure

setting . . . A scene, perhaps, from Grandmother's porch —
spruce trees unthreading memory's bruised sky, smoke
from a chimney, the distance in yellow strands against a back-
drop of dark air; it could be your father on a sled looking
up from Ohio, though it's you in your new snowsuit, waving
into the lens in Springfield, eyes squinting from the cold

as if only half awake. Or it could be the coast of California,
fog advancing its limbo beyond the window, dissolving
the lemon fields inch by inch as you practice that Bach
etude each Saturday — double pennants, whole and quarter
notes, half-filled moons blind-eyed as fish in the dankest
ocean depth. Whatever became of those scores, bass and

treble clefs curled tight as shells — the signatures of time
on the staffs, tidal striations, sea tunes in the wash and low
rumble, the grey matter of the skull? Did they sink back
earthward from the rafters with a dusty chorusing of the dead,
or are they still carried out on the starlight's long glissandi?
and all that science — Sidereal Time measured by a motion

between stars we can't really see, out there in the crossing
patterns of their beams — what will it finally mean given
the evaporation all about us, that process we duplicated in lab
vials and tubes? Flick of the bunsen burner and water shimmered
into steam — stop the end up, and it fell back in grey notes
too heavy for the air to hold, as if change could be reversed,

as if, all things being equal before our eyes, we didn't wonder
if cloud-like we would form again, and in light or darkness
rain down in another life. And the sea going up, molecule
by molecule around us — the soul then perhaps nothing more
than a glass of ocean water, salty and indistinctly blue
as it escapes our essential dust. And Einstein tells us that

light is generally unsourced in the universe, and if
we were to ever travel at that speed, we would be light,
break apart and randomly disperse into the dead weight
of eternity. How much of all of this then lies up inside
the heart, spins in on itself like a great accretion disc, a dim
silt that increasingly becomes us, blots us finally out?

And here, another autumn's end and few birds flying
on the dusk, the blank humming of the air taking us
closer to that day when atom by atom we'll disappear without
a sound. I think about the feeder hung on our back porch
and the house finch, having mistaken the window for nothing,
knocked cold next to it — for three full minutes, within the dark

cradle of my hands, I kept it warm in its unconscious breath
before it came to and flew off into what might have seemed
another life. Now, as the first stars branch out and the night
quickens all about us and rises, it's no wonder that I'm more
content than ever to spend time just sitting among the dead
leaves, the shadows and immediate metaphysics of the trees.

AFTER A THEME BY VALLEJO, AFTER A THEME BY JUSTICE

for Jon Veinberg

It will come for me in Florence with the evening light, and on account
of the light, in early autumn before the rainstorms have arrived —
when the *sfumato,* that smoke of rose and saffron, has so overrun the air
that my worn heart, poor moth, will want to take up after the profligate
clouds, their violet sinking toward the west. It will find me, once more
extending my stay for no reason beyond the light, known far too well
by the vinaios, in the little places for soup — on a day when I am little more
than another narrow shadow on Borgo Santi Apostoli or Via dele Terme,
my body dependent on a stick, but I will not be tired of this, for even
though my shoulders press against the brick, and I have no clue,
my eyes will be at attention, thinking that the road is still ahead.

Doubtless a Sunday with its poor excuses for an afternoon — the trattorias dark,
the tourist couples gone from goldsmiths' shops on the Ponte Vecchio.
A Sunday like all the others when I've made my way early to the loggia
for the open sun in the fountain, to sit again and admire the statues,
those palpable, undiminished shapes, and that smooth, colossal beauty
in marble-perfect clouds that saunter down each noon from Fiesole —
both reminding us of a life surpassing our own, both headed one way
or the other in time. And what will it matter then if I have a smoke,
comforted as I will be by the company of these white choirs of air
and stone, their long and brilliant reflection on it all. And earlier,
at that point where the standard-bearing cart halted on its way back
from battle, I will have stopped in the mercato, and out of respect, and
again for luck, I'll have rubbed the bronze snout of the Porcillino.

Then, I will make my way by heart to the Baptistry where the symbolism
of black marble pressed alongside white will not have escaped me,
where I will admire once more Ghiberti's self portrait among the panels,
the bald humility of his head there on the Gates of Paradise, and looking
much the same, I'll envy him his dull, protracted shining. And the sun
will be bright then in the camera lenses of tourists, as atop the Duomo
they focus toward Giotto's Campanile — the white, green, and terra cotta
marbles blanching in that aureate stream, and the shade sliding down
Ghiberti's burnished doors, and the tales about this world will once more be
old tales, still lacking a little in perspective just like the blue above me
when it's stripped down to a red flaming along the roofs and river banks,
when the surface of the Arno is brazed for an hour or so with gold, as I
head up the hillside to my room in the soggiorno, There I'll finally lean

across the window sill and not step aside as the far clouds fade along
that road on which each of us is at last alone. And I might think then
of Michelangelo at ninety despairing of all the world, of all his great art,
flayed as he was with God, with the knotted ropes, the sticks of time;
and for a moment I, too, might think, unwittingly, that I've seen it all.

But then I may well recall my friend in a place as strange and far away
as Fresno, too old, after all, to know any better than to ride his bicycle,
recklessly on sidewalks by the thrift shops and Basque hotels, trying
the patience of folks at the fruit stands and used-books stalls, smiling
his great Baltic teeth at no one he recognizes any more, pedaling slowly
home past the one revival theater still showing films in black and white.
I think I'll be able to picture it as he puts his feet up on his front porch,
and though he's sworn it off, he'll pour himself a water glass of wine
red as an autumn sun burning low through the sycamores, and for no reason
better than the end of another day, he'll drink to a deep and cloudless sky.

SPECULATION IN DARK AIR

Twilight was a short burn before the blue
bruise a day wears into — autumn ending,
tossing its black trees low against the sky,
the shoulders of the air slumped a bit, gone
ochre at the dim earth's blunted edge . . .

And this week the first fusilade of snow
flakes blowing in, all at once, the way stars
ambush this backdrop, this blank calyx,
and, apparitional, burst through the deep
azures to blink on before that absolute

rising of the night. But tonight the stars
sit out, neglected, benign, softly whirling
we know now, at the heart of nothing
so unknowable as we once thought — these
bright spinning islands no longer endless

in the stream, for we've finally tracked down
the limits of the envelope — the vast immeasurable
squared off, the universe now knotted somewhere
like the end of a long black balloon. But for all
our intents and purposes there's the infinite

latitude and vacancy of the dark, which is still
expanding, and billions of light-years are free
to unravel before it runs out. Yet everything
is more finite than before, as our best guesses go
mystically where this nothing ends, the other side

of all there is: and if space is curved, then curved
on what? Not even the proverbial thin air . . .
Big Bang, Unified Field Theory, these attractive
reasonings collapse everything back to that first
clapping of the cosmic hand, but come up short

against this new unbounded breathlessness,
or some immaterial wall that stops the last rondo
of our stars. This entire effect may be its own
cause. Even so, old questions have their weight —
What's beyond the vortex of our days? What stuff

if not the quick stuff we're made of? Whatever
is left of innocence must be ours, as we peek out
beneath the clouds, self-consciously arranging
the sky to explain each brilliance amid our sense
of loss — we would have the stars resemble us,

like the Japanese who send lanterns out to sea
to guide the souls . . . Or like, on one of the world's
highest lakes, the fishermen of Patzcuaro, Mexico,
who in their thin canoes skim the glassy surface
for the star-white and almost transparent fish

and, holding out cloud-like butterfly nets fully
in their arms, dip to the water as clouds pass by,
almost as if they were fishing only for those
quiet clouds. Perhaps they believe their hearts fill
with clouds or that at last they'll become clouds

and lift above it all, tied loosely to the slow
movement of this life and so not lost forever
to the world? They're content in what they know
and have no long-range fears beyond the sky.
Yet how much of this is sleight of hand, lost

in mirrors, the shifting opacities of the mind?
The mean distance to M 31 is 2.2 million light-years;
in the 30's it was 750,000 — an easy oversight, given
our atmosphere's jaded scrim, the interstellar rain
of dusts. Each half century, facts change, as if physics

were just a matter of style; but by the time
we could ever tell of this star's death, of its im-
plosion to light-soaking cinders, we'd have fanned
out in our solar winds, countless among the black,
ameobic tides. Even now it could be burnt-out,

and what we have arriving is an unsourced drive
of light, the window dressing of the past in sus-
pended present tense? Everything being relative,
galaxies grow tired before our eyes, weary finally
in their floss and chorus. And though there's nowhere

else for us but in the rucksack of our flesh, though
we stare boldly to Andromeda or the Corona Borealis,
our breath sends up its small white flags, ultimately
surrendering our airy conceits, as we stand on this side
of the dark, shivering like the grass or like the stars.

DARK TIME

Snow all day until
the sky is a falling
stasis — time mounting up
like the ice in windy swirls,
in spiraled, barred or elliptical
galaxies across the window glass;
and the dim caul of air
like that star cloud
so dense it blocks
our view to the center
of the Milky Way.
           And so
I finally have hours to do
nothing but settle back
and remember what it was
exactly I used to be
so obsessed about — what went
climbing out of my heart
pure as the purple flames
of bougainvillaea up the sun-
bleached stucco of my youth?

But my mind draws blanks,
like one of those radio dishes
in the deserts of New Mexico
that's trained on the deep
and abstract heart of space
on a day when only static
interference is skimmed off stars.

I should be tracing out
thoughts like the scientist
at a telescope during "dark time" —
those nights when the moon is down
and the least heavenly body
ignites on the photo plates —
the lost spark and slow burn,
flotsam of matter's first wreck still
blasting by the floorboards of time.
He plays dot-to-dot, looking for

a little linkage, some new move-
ment across the firmament's
held breath by which he might
name the unknown, say
it's a shiny grain smaller,
somewhat like the light beams
we've divided down to quarks
and neutrinos, all these small
threads coming loose off
the long sleeves of the dark.
But I sit here passive
as any receiver, silent
as the cogwheels of the void
grinding blindly away, barely
vital as that dust and star floss
lifted just enough into our air
so we might appreciate the light.

I think I like it better
the way Aristotle had it —
all the planets pushed around
the perfect earth by angels
on concentric crystal spheres,
everything self-referential,
parochial as the blue.
Even the Egyptians and Chinese
saw stars as little lamps
set out at the same distance
from the earth, though each
deciphered different animals crawling
in the light's bare bones.

Memories are often like this
group of asteroids discovered
bumping about the belt
between Jupiter and Mars;
darker than anthracite, no brightness
going out from them as they bob
and weave among ice and refraction,
tear away and are known only

by a bulge in the force fields
around planets or moons.

And staring now out this grey
glass, I catch on my reflection,
and I recall that time when I was twelve,
the cabinet mirrors on each side
of the bathroom sink tilting
out enough so I could see
my face duplicate and recede,
framed smaller back to a pinpoint
in space until I closed my eyes
only to hear in that darkness
the unconscious march of Latin
drilled into my brain, the ancient
certainty of the dead proclaiming
new and conquered boundaries.
But, when I opened my eyes,
I saw the same rainclouds
that kept me in all day, holding
there like dull frescoes on a wall,
like thumbprints in ash — only
a remote glimmer of intention
behind the confines of the sky.

APOLOGUES OF WINTER LIGHT

Street lamps streaming on, and the grey
suspiration of the cold flossing the invisible
tides of air, full with all our lost breath . . .

Soon the heavens will span out — and though
I've learned everything is falling outward,
the galaxies still come set like pin feathers
spired on the dark's spread wings . . .

This time of year, before a brief twilight
turns away, I think of Tiepolo's cherubim,
all countenance and wing, bodiless among
the clouded wisps, breaking away, floating
off like anything souls might be — I think
of our lives drifting out there, too, like slow
light through these blue and trembling trees.

Only a hundred thousand years ago
mastodons grazed in Central Park,
and the constellations spun over them
gently as shining leaves — the dark pools,
the staves of ice singing back the mild
ostinato of the stars . . .
                              We've tried to figure
our place in the far backwaters and
sequinned outskirts of time, tried to pin down
that one background note reverberating
even in the rocks. But the tumbling
geometry of the sky resolves little more
than those chiseled blocks of light,
those overlays of rust and amber
that were all of an autumn thickening
the air, absolving some distance until we felt
we could take that burning it into us.
                              Nonetheless,
I'm watching Venus rise through the diminished
atmosphere of New Jersey, red as a maple leaf
I've taped above the window to keep my hope
in perspective, for still I'm not much beyond
that feeling at age two when my father,

on a fire escape in east Missouri, lifted me
into the cool, blue night of the 50's,
and I pointed saying, *moon, moon,*
as it basked there large and white
as a beach ball spinning just beyond
my arm's reach . . .

                And each year now
we know more, but we know no better —
what we see in the sky is simply
the softened gloss of the past sifting
back to us, and likewise, every atom
down the body's shining length
was inside a star, and will be again.

DARK MATTER

Beneath the music from a farther room.
T.S. Eliot

Drawn out past
our local orbits,
past street lamps pushing
the night back beyond
a walkway's sleeping roses
and the cul-de-sac,
we are once more
none the wiser
unearthed in the fact
that ninety percent of the universe
is not radiating? All the non-
luminous chaff tossed off
the kernels of light — all that
is really most all of it
as things now add up
and will not appear.

I've arrived at middle age
in a moonless month,
and though the heavens are clearer
for that, I'm still seining
among the stars without a clue.
But somewhere, it's out there,
chockablock about the blue
and unfathomable fire
of quasars, dodging
crab nebulae, white dwarfs —
so many black asterisks bobbing
in the dimples of gravity,
the relative bend and sink holes
of space.
        As far as I can see
it's as if the cosmos were
ten percent music, a leitmotif
or glossy harmony
spun out against the dread-
naught of silence. Life slipped

in somewhere, sparkling,
say, on the tenth-notes —
one metronomic pause
between the red-shift of galaxies,
a few white notes, reversed
out on the black cosmic sheet,
composing the only music
we have ever made sense of.
Mozart, you heard it said,
took dictation from the stars,
progressions of chords, arias and
divertimento arriving transfixed
in his mind as the constellations
first inscribed by the Chaldeans.

* * *

After dinner, the pinwheel
of the Milky Way uncoils
its spangled shirttails across
the back lots of a universe
ten billion light-years end to
end — and now when looking out,
I picture that distance
like a luminous clothesline
upon which all blind space is hung,
though we've long been told
that it's all brilliance, all
radiance and a shower of light
at the end . . .
                    For now,
our thoughts could be nothing
more than asteroids, circling
the fission of the mind — sand,
boulders, small worlds; the lost,
the faint, the fresh as blood —
silica, carbonacious compounds,
nickel and iron — everything
we might be or all we'll never
become. Yet whatever it is
we've done shines often, persists,

and comes back to us like comets
slowly wearing down on their
icy and elliptical tracks.
It all hangs with us, a worry
in the air — spalls of cold light
scudding among the turgid
gravel of the dark.
                    Perhaps
like bits of smoky celluloid,
negatives with their pale-
as-paper figures, we wait to be
held up once more against
a brightness to begin again?

Or perhaps it's that we drift
airily around star to star,
their billion silver keys
every brilliance there is to tell —
that jangling all the obsequies
we will ever hear?
                    Maybe
this is why I go for walks
more often now at night,
whistling some tune
I dimly recall,
if only for distraction's sake,
for the circumstantial evidence
of my breath with its faint
refraction of star dross
bright in a cloud before me . . .

MIDLIFE

Because out of nowhere one day
the grace disappeared
from my body, rarely to be seen
again except in that unconscious
wrist-snap of a racket head
as it kicks out the side-
ways arc of an American twist,
I went out for my birthday and,
instead of a Cos d'Estournel '82,
bought two Day-Glo green-and-
yellow parakeets, some seed,
cuttle bone, and cage,
along with a flagon of something
truly unremarkable
from Czechoslovakia.

We carried them finger to cage,
these frank dispositions, attended
as an inflated chatter proclaimed
their vibrant devotion to the air.
We spoke to them much as if they were
autistic children, capable somehow
of one spectacular, clear feat — as if,
being simple, they were simply loved —
as if, perhaps, they might take the place
of children, had one wanted children . . .

*

And this year, players in the Series
looked younger than ever before, all
of them — even stodgy catchers
who hadn't shaved. And never have I
been so attentive to weather —
where the jet stream might drag
down the clouds, road ice, airport delays —
as if there were something to be done.
I especially enjoy the channel that shows
temperatures in Barcelona or in Rome
superimposed on postcard vistas
so starched with sunlight that when

I close my eyes I'm walking the Ramblas
or the Corso, or off praising one tree
or another in the Jardin des Plantes.
Or I see the supple lace of jacarandas,
the deep-iris sky over Montecito —
my legs were somehow then attached
to the tireless direction of the breeze,
as unconcerned as the itinerant clouds.

Now I notice most my friends
have rowing machines or stationary
bikes, and I have bought a fancy one
on time, the kind with a dashboard
of lights and beeps like a starship,
one with a computer read-out for hills,
levels, duration, intensity, RPMs.
It's called a Life Cycle, and there's not
a minute goes by that the irony is lost
on me. It's the kind I used to warm up
on in the mirrored gym before running
or workouts on the weight machines —
but lately I walk by refusing
to even glance at it, hamstrung
by a flagging affinity for pain.

Nonetheless, I have not taken to
wearing a cardigan or bow tie,
nor have I insisted students
call me Dr. or Professor, this or that . . .
Because next year, when I get my grant,
I'm heading for the coast and home —
going to buy one of those old big boards
and, without one thought for carcinoma,
stay all day long in the surf, nose-riding,
shooting the curl on shoulder-high sets
like nobody's business. And on Fridays
I'm going to hit an Italian restaurant
I know and eat rigatoni like Tony Quinn
in that old Fellini film, drink a few
water glasses of red wine with friends

and walk out late into starlight, into the blue
and immutable sea sounds of the past.

And nowadays, more and more in dreams
I'm flying — just taking off from the side-
walk mid-conversation, pushing the air
back like water with my hands, the way
I remember learning to dog paddle
in the Pacific, bobbing then above the azure
levels in the world. It's simple, something
I always knew, but something larger,
more elementary than all the images
of parochial school, something hidden
like the white and floating hearts of saints,
something I had just forgotten all this time —
a little transcendental muscle gone soft
but coming back, some instant weight-loss
plan. I rise then effortlessly above
the cypress and eucalyptus trees,
and there I am, suddenly once more
gliding over that sea cliff and the coast
for as long as I can remember . . .